Standing Stones

Steve Marshall

IMPORTANT DATES

	Mesolithic	**8000 BC** 8,500 BC: Post holes at Stonehenge

Occupation of Blick Mead, near Stonehenge: 8,000–3,000 BC

4000 BC

First occupation of the Boyne Valley, Ireland: 4,000 BC

4,000–3,000 BC: Dolmens constructed in Britain

West Kennet long barrow, Wiltshire: 3,670 BC

3,700 BC: Construction of long barrows begins in Britain

First stone rows on Dartmoor, Cornwall: 3,500 BC

3,500 BC: First stone circles constructed in Britain

Boyne Valley passage tombs (Newgrange etc.), Ireland: 3,300 BC

3,300 BC: Earliest structures at Ness of Brodgar, Orkney

3,200 BC: Castlerigg stone circle, Cumbria

Stones of Stenness, Orkney : 3,000 BC

3,000 BC: Rollright Stones, Oxfordshire

Stanton Drew, Somerset: 3,000 BC

3,000 BC: Earthworks at Stonehenge & Avebury, Wiltshire

Main structures at Ness of Brodgar, Orkney: 2,900 BC

2,900–2,600 BC: Callanish Stones, Isle of Lewis

Chambered tombs on Anglesey, Wales: 2,700 BC

2,700 BC: Maeshowe, Orkney

Stonehenge stones erected: 2,620–2,480 BC

2,600–2,000 BC: Avebury stones erected

Ring of Brodgar, Orkney: 2,600 BC

2,600 BC: Construction of round barrows begins in Britain

Great Pyramid, Egypt: 2,560 BC

2500 BC

1,500 BC: Drombeg stone circle, Ireland

Stone circles abandoned: 1,000 BC

800 BC

43 AD

Timeline bar (top to bottom): Mesolithic, Neolithic, Bronze Age, Iron Age

INTRODUCTION

In Britain and Ireland there is an extraordinary concentration and diversity of prehistoric standing stones, also known as megaliths ('large stones'). The earliest known stones were erected in the Neolithic period some 6,000 years ago; throughout the Bronze Age the custom continued, finally coming to an end in the Iron Age, roughly 3,000 years ago. There are stones that stand alone, and stones arranged in rows, circles or other patterns. Some were used to construct tombs and other structures; all may be loosely termed 'monuments'. Throughout Britain there are prehistoric monumental landscapes, such as Avebury, where an assortment of monuments may be scattered across an area several miles across.

Some of Britain's megalithic monuments are internationally famous and have become major tourist attractions. However, there are hundreds more that are little known and not always easy to find, despite being marked on Ordnance Survey maps. Some stand conspicuously on hilltops and are visible from far away; others may be hidden in valleys and woodland. Hunting for standing stones can be great fun and often introduces us to stunning scenery, leading us into new landscapes that we might not otherwise have thought to explore.

The Men-an-Tol (meaning 'holed stone') near Penzance in Cornwall is thought to date to either the late Neolithic or early Bronze Age.

SINGLE STONES

Single standing stones, or menhirs, are found all over the British Isles. At more than 7.6 metres (25 feet) high, the tallest is the Rudston Monolith in Yorkshire. Once the focus of a vast, Neolithic monumental landscape, the monolith today rises incongruously close to a Norman church, built several thousand years after the stone was raised. An 18th-century investigator determined that there is as much of the stone beneath the ground as above, and found many buried human skulls as he dug. Made of gritstone, the stone has an indentation that could be a dinosaur's footprint. It comes from a source over ten miles away; if not moved by people, it could have been transported to Rudston by glacier.

All around Britain there are stones that have been moved from one region to another by glaciers during successive ice ages. When the glaciers melted and retreated the stones were left behind, sometimes hundreds of miles from their origin. Known as glacial erratics, these stones must have

Kintraw Menhir Kilmartin.

The Rudston Monolith.

Macleods Stone Harris.

been regarded as special by prehistoric people, since they were so different to the local stones. Some were honoured, or 'monumentalised', by being mounted vertically in the ground.

Single standing stones are sometimes found sited at a distance from stone circles. Known as outliers, they are thought to have had an astronomical function – perhaps marking significant positions of the sun, moon or stars, as viewed from the circle (*see p.15*).

(*see p.15*).

Carbon-dating.

Standing stones may have been erected for a variety of reasons: as memorials, as route-markers, or to indicate land boundaries. Though most are ancient, others may have been erected relatively recently. Dating the stone settings is not easy – modern carbon-dating can be extremely accurate, but will only work with organic material, not stone. If a stone has fallen, material from beneath it may produce accurate dating, but such an opportunity is rare. It is not uncommon to find dateable human remains and pottery buried close to a stone, but they may have been deposited long after it was erected. The technique of luminescence-dating may sometimes be used to determine when a buried stone was last exposed to light or heat.

STONE ROWS/AVENUES

Merrivale stone row on Dartmoor.

Dating mostly from the Late Neolithic and Early Bronze Ages, some standing stones are arranged in long, mostly straight rows. Often there are several rows running in parallel. A double row, made of two parallel lines of stones, is termed an avenue. Stone rows can be found in Scandinavia, and notably in France; the most impressive are in Carnac, Brittany, which has over 3,000 stones. Some of the Carnac stones were erected as early as 4,500 BC.

British stone rows are typically found in isolated areas of moorland, and there are many on Dartmoor. The longest stone row in Britain (and possibly the world) is Upper Erme – a single row made of over 900 stones of different sizes. Far from straight, it runs broadly north–south across the moor for over two miles and crosses a river. Along the course of the row are several cairns, and at its southern end is a stone circle.

There are several short stone rows in Wales and Ireland. Scotland has around 20, all in Caithness and northern Sutherland. Ballymeanoch in the Kilmartin Glen

has six stones surviving from what was once a much longer avenue. Most Scottish monuments typically have more than six rows of rather small stones that radiate in a fan shape from one central point. The Hill o' Many Stanes is the best-known example.

From the vast stone circle of Avebury, in Wiltshire, runs the West Kennet Avenue – a double row of huge sarsen stones. Partially restored in the 1930s, the Avenue ranges over the landscape for half a mile, but it may once have run on for another mile. Avebury originally had another avenue, of which only two stones now remain.

Why did prehistoric people build stone rows? Numerous astronomical theories have been proposed, and there may be astronomical elements in some designs, but there are strong indications that what the builders were interested in was water. The stone rows on landlocked Dartmoor, for instance, almost all have views of the sea, even though it is as much as 12 miles away. The rows are usually sited near, or point to, springs and river confluences; many other British sites, too, indicate that water was extremely important in prehistory. Did water symbolise the 'otherworld'? Perhaps stone rows and avenues were symbolic rivers, along which the souls of the dead were conveyed to larger rivers, and ultimately to the sea?

West Kennet Avenue.

Newgrange Stone Row.

STONE CIRCLES

Boscawen-un.

The British Isles are home to an enormous number of stone circles, the earliest dating back to 3,500 BC. Despite the ravages of time, weather and wilful destruction, more than 1,300 circles still survive today; at one time there must have been many times that number. Stone circles vary enormously in every respect – some are not even circular, but oval. Most stone monuments are made from local materials, though sometimes an unusual stone regarded as 'special' may have been transported from a few miles away to enhance the circle. The number of stones in a circle ranges from four to around 100, though the commonest number is 12. Few circles are in pristine condition, though, and stones may have been removed, or even added, over the centuries.

Most stone circles measure less than 30 metres in diameter, with the smallest at only two or three metres. At the other end of the scale is Avebury, the world's largest stone circle, at almost a quarter of a mile across.

Nine Maidens Bronze Age stone circle on Dartmoor.

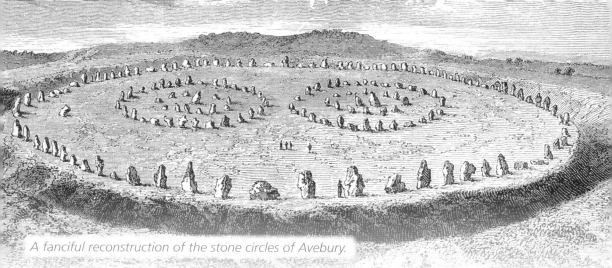

A fanciful reconstruction of the stone circles of Avebury.

Why were stone circles built? Some circles appear to be aligned to positions on the horizon that mark the rising or setting of heavenly bodies. Others have evidence of ceremonial use – in rare cases, a circular groove has been etched into the ground by dancers' feet. It is quite possible that some stone circles were used as calendars.

Many circles may have been multifunctional – their use as, say, a calendar would probably be linked to astronomy, and they could still be used for meetings and ceremonies. The builders of Stonehenge evidently had sophisticated astronomical knowledge, and many claim the structure to be a 'computer' capable of predicting eclipses; yet there is also evidence that Stonehenge was used for funerary rituals and burials.

In north-west Scotland around 70 recumbent stone circles can be found; there are several more in south-west Ireland. In these circles most of the stones are mounted vertically, but one stone lies horizontal (recumbent). The builders went to a great deal of trouble to make the top face of this recumbent stone perfectly level with the horizon. At midsummer in northern latitudes the full moon does not set, but skims low over the horizon, then rises again. Recumbent stones are positioned so that the moon passes over the stone when viewed from the centre of the circle. In some circles small pieces of white, shiny quartz were scattered over the ground in front of the recumbent stone to reflect the moonlight and enhance the effect.

Grange SC Lough Gur.

DOLMENS (QUOITS)

A variety of dolmens.

Of all Britain's megalithic monuments, dolmens are the most enigmatic. Human remains and artefacts, ideal for carbon-dating, have been found buried close to dolmens, but these are of little use for dating the monuments, since they may have been deposited long after the stones were erected. Most British dolmens, however, are thought to date from the early Neolithic period (4,000–3,000 BC). Similar monuments, some of them a thousand years older, are found all across Western Europe.

Also known as quoits, dolmens are found particularly around the fringes of the Irish Sea – in Wales, south-east Ireland, Devon and Cornwall. Each consists of a large, flat stone slab, or capstone, raised up on two or more stone uprights. In Cornwall capstones tend to be fairly thin slabs, set at an angle; in Ireland they are usually heavy blocks, some more than a metre thick, set flat. The Blackstone in Co. Carlow, Ireland, is Europe's largest dolmen, with a capstone estimated to weigh an incredible 150 tonnes. The structures we see today, however, are rather like skeletons, since most dolmens were once covered with earth or stones and resembled round barrows or cairns.

Trethevy Quoit.

Lanyon Quoit.

Trethevy Quoit.

PRE-LOVED: STONES INCORPORATED INTO LATER MONUMENTS

Maeshowe on the island of Orkney is a magnificent chambered tomb, dating from around 2,700 BC. Inside this large grass-covered mound is a complex structure of stone, with passages and chambers. Archaeologists suspect that the site may initially

have been a house, then a stone circle, before the present monument was built. Inside Maeshowe's central chamber are four huge megaliths that are thought to have come from the stone circle.

There are many examples of reused megaliths across the British Isles. The famous 'bluestones' of Stonehenge originate from the Preseli Hills in Wales, 150 miles away. Before being set in their present positions, the

Interior chamber of Maeshowe.

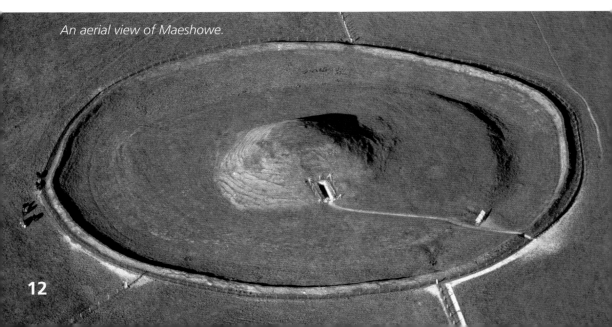

An aerial view of Maeshowe.

90 or so bluestones are thought to have been rearranged several times. Some may have been used first to build a circle of 28 stones by the River Avon, a mile from Stonehenge. If this theory is correct, the stone circle was later dismantled and its stones moved to Stonehenge, to be used with others in several different arrangements that were changed over the centuries. It has been suggested that some of the bluestones may have been used in a monument in Wales, before they even got to Stonehenge.

The West Kennet long barrow, near Avebury, was built around 3,670 BC, but some of the sarsen stones used in its construction show signs of earlier use. Before they were erected in the monument, the hard, abrasive stones had been laid flat and used for polishing stone axes. Characteristic polishing marks can be seen on several of the stones – one has a long, flat groove. Other stones have smaller polishing areas that are smooth as glass.

Polishing marks evident at the West Kennet long barrow.

Early Christians sometimes adopted former prehistoric sites that had been abandoned, constructing churches on them and even incorporating megaliths into the new building. One standing stone is now built into a pub. The Oxenham Arms in South Zeal, Devon, has an enormous menhir inside it: parts of the pub are believed to be the remains of a former 12th-century Benedictine monastery that was built around the menhir. The stone is now in the snug bar, where it extends up the wall from floor to ceiling. It continues up and beyond, through to the next floor, where it projects five feet into one of the guest bedrooms. Reportedly, the stone is rooted 14 feet into the ground. Cut from local Dartmoor granite, it is estimated to weigh 17 tonnes.

The exposed central section of the South Zeal Menhir. Unusually it is positioned not in soft ground, but in shale rock, which would have needed to be cut out in order to place the stone vertically.

FOLKLORE

A giant helps Merlin build Stonehenge.

There are many myths and legends attached to standing stones: some say they were made by giants.

The Merry Maidens, and similarly titled stone circles, usually take their name from a legendary group of young girls who danced on the Sabbath and were turned to stone for their sins. If there is an outlier stone, it is said to be the piper or fiddler who played for the dancers. The victims were not always deliberately wicked: in some versions of the tale they danced late on a Saturday night and accidentally continued past midnight.

A common myth is that standing stones occasionally move at night, going down to the nearest river to drink. They do this only at certain times, such as New Year's Eve. Megalithic monuments are often sited near rivers and springs, whose water levels fluctuate seasonally. In winter the waters rise and may flood to meet the stones, so this myth could well be based on fact.

The Merry Maidens Neolithic stone circle near St Buryan in the far west of Cornwall.

ASTRONOMY

Prehistoric people had knowledge of the movements of the sun, moon and stars, which they sometimes applied in constructing megalithic monuments. Some of these monuments seem to be aligned to positions on the horizon where heavenly bodies rise and set. But the night sky today is not as it appeared 5,000 years ago: the positions of all the stars have shifted considerably. The sun and moon have shifted only slightly, but we still need to use computers to calculate alignments accurately, rather than simply observing.

Alignments are difficult to prove, since they could be accidental. A line of standing stones may point in either of two directions, so how do we know which one mattered? For centuries people have admired the famous Stonehenge alignment, flocking to view the midsummer sunrise from the monument. Evidence, though, suggests that Stonehenge's builders were more concerned with the alignment to the midwinter sunset – in exactly the opposite direction.

Star trails over the Ring of Brodgar.

The best evidence for accurate prehistoric alignments can be found in megalithic chambered tombs, constructed more than 5,000 years ago. At Newgrange in Ireland, for several weeks around the winter solstice the rising sun shines down a narrow 19-metre-long passage to illuminate a chamber at its end. Maeshowe on Orkney is similarly designed. At the winter solstice Maeshowe's end chamber is lit by the sun, not as it rises, but as it sets. There is little room for spectators in the chambers, and bad weather often obscures the sun, so the events are broadcast live on the internet.

Newgrange.

STONEHENGE

Stonehenge trilithon.

Set in the wide, open landscape of Salisbury Plain, Stonehenge lies at the centre of a greater monumental landscape many miles across. The iconic circle of huge, lintelled sarsen stones surrounds the much smaller bluestones and central towering trilithons.

Sometime around 8,000 BC, Mesolithic hunter-gatherers erected a line of huge pine 'totem poles' close to where the Stonehenge circle stands today; the same people were to occupy Blick Mead, a nearby area of warm springs, for the next 4,500 years.

Neolithic people began to construct monuments from about 3,500 BC, starting with the Greater Cursus – a vast linear earthwork almost two miles long. At Durrington, a couple of miles north-east of Stonehenge, there was a large settlement of substantial houses; it was probably here that the builders of Stonehenge lived.

In around 3,000 BC a circular bank and ditch was built; today it surrounds the stones. Just within it the 56 Aubrey Holes were dug. These were used to deposit cremations, and may once have held the Welsh bluestones. Alignments to the complex motions of the moon are apparent in this early version of Stonehenge.

Work continued, with several changes of plan and possibly a change of beliefs: when the sarsen stones were erected around 2,500 BC, they were aligned not to the moon, but to the sun. Five great trilithons were arranged in a horseshoe, open to the north-east. Each upright was more than six metres tall, weighing 35–40 tonnes. Around them, 30 more sarsens, each

Sunrise at Stonehenge.

4.1 metres high and weighing 20 tonnes, were erected in a circle, supporting 30 lintels. The stones were smoothed and made squarer, with carved mortise and tenon joints holding the lintel stones in place. The circle of lintels was made perfectly horizontal. Stonehenge's sarsens are widely assumed to have been transported from the Marlborough Downs, 25 miles away, although there is no evidence for this.

Like other monumental landscapes of the late Neolithic period, the Stonehenge area has a strong connection with water. From Stonehenge's north-eastern entrance runs an 'avenue' – a slightly raised earthwork nearly two miles long. The Avenue turns east, and then veers south-east to meet the River Avon in a marshy area of springs. It is thought that some of the bluestones once stood there as a stone circle before being relocated to the main Stonehenge site.

AVEBURY

Sited on the North Wiltshire Downs, in one of Britain's most recognisable monumental landscapes, the great stone circle of Avebury is truly enormous. A quarter of a mile across, it is made of gigantic sarsen stones, erected in about 2,500 BC. The great circle once had around 100 stones; within it were two smaller circles of about 30 stones each. Surrounding the circle is a massive henge – a nine-metre-deep ditch with an outer bank.

The monument had four entrances, which today have roads passing through them; inside the circle is a village, with shops and a pub. From two of the entrances, double rows of standing stones ran for several miles across the landscape. One of these – the West Kennet Avenue – has been partially restored, but of the other avenue only two stones survive.

An aerial view of the stones at Avebury.

West Kennet Avenue at Avebury on a frosty morning.

Avebury fell into ruin, with many of its stones toppled in the medieval period and buried. In the 1700s more of its stones were broken into pieces and used for building. It was partly restored in the 1930s by Alexander Keiller, a millionaire with a passion for archaeology. Keiller bought Avebury and used his personal fortune to try to return it to its former glory. Eventually, money and time ran out, and work was halted due to the outbreak of war in 1939.

Like the sarsens of Stonehenge, Avebury's stones have long been assumed to have been transported from the nearby Marlborough Downs, where vast natural 'drifts' cover the ground. But the Avebury stones are not all the same: they are not the uniform grey colour that they first appear to be, but come in a variety of colours, shapes and thicknesses. The stones must come from several sources – from distinctly different 'batches' of sarsen.

It is likely that Avebury's largest surviving stones, all weighing between 70 and 100 tonnes each, were formed naturally, very close to where they are today, and that because they were regarded as 'special', the henge's earthwork was built around them. The other stones in the circle are considerably smaller and may have been gathered from several sources outside the henge, where sarsen was plentiful. Up until the early 19th century the landscape surrounding Avebury had many drifts of sarsen stone, but they were removed for use as building material.

NESS OF BRODGAR

Near the centre of Mainland, the largest of the Orkney Islands, is a thin strip of land known as the Ness of Brodgar; only a few hundred metres wide, it is bordered by two lochs. At either end of the Ness are two spectacular stone circles: the Standing Stones of Stenness and the Ring of Brodgar, dating from around 3,000 BC and 2,600 BC respectively.

Originally a henge monument (possibly the oldest in Britain), the Standing Stones of Stenness later became a stone circle of probably 12 stones. Four of its towering, angular stones survive. Up to five metres high, they are wide, thin slabs of local Orkney flagstone. Surrounded by a ditch cut into the rock, the stones were erected on an artificially levelled platform. Outside the circle stands a 5.6-metre-high outlier known as the Watch Stone.

At the other end of the Ness is the Ring of Brodgar, 104 metres (341 feet) in diameter. Although also described as a henge, it has no outer bank. Brodgar's encircling ditch, six metres wide, was cut three metres deep into the sandstone bedrock – a task that must have taken enormous time and effort. The ring is thought to have originally had 60 stones, of which only 27 survive today.

The Stones of Stenness.

The Ring of Brodgar.

An aerial view of the Ness of Brodgar.

Though considerably smaller than the Stones of Stenness, the megaliths are still impressive, standing between 2.1 and 4.7 metres high. Made of blue-grey Orkney flagstone slabs, some have vivid orange stripes on their short sides. Orkney flagstone, like slate, is laminated and splits easily into thin sheets. One of the Brodgar megaliths was split in two by a lightning strike in 1980: one half still stands; the other lies fallen beside it. Perhaps more of the stones were lost this way.

In between these two stone circles lies an area of ongoing archaeological excavations of tremendous importance. Archaeologists are slowly revealing a large complex of monumental Neolithic stone buildings, unparalleled in Britain for their scale and sophistication.

The earliest buildings, dating from 3,300 BC, have not yet been excavated – they were overlaid with other structures throughout a period of occupation lasting a thousand years. One building from 2,900 BC has been described as a 'Neolithic Cathedral'. Its massive stone walls are four metres (13 feet) thick and in its centre is a cross-shaped inner sanctum. A standing stone with a hole is built into one of the walls. As work continues we will certainly learn more about this site and those who lived there.

The archaeological dig at the Ness of Brodgar site.

CALLANISH (CALANAIS)

On the Isle of Lewis, in the Outer Hebrides, is one of Britain's best-preserved megalithic structures. Overlooking Loch Roag is the Callanish Stones – an impressive arrangement of megaliths, shaped like a Celtic cross with a stone circle at its centre. There are many smaller stone circles and other megaliths in this monumental landscape, all with the usual connection to water.

The Callanish Stones.

Seen in silhouette, many of the Callanish Stones resemble cloaked human figures or animals. The 13 stones of the circle average three metres in height; at the circle's centre is a single thin slab 4.8 metres high. From the circle a single row of stones runs due south for 27 metres, and a double row runs roughly north for 83 metres, with short single rows of stones running east and west. Archaeoastronomers have found several alignments to the sun and moon in the Callanish Stones and some believe the site to have been a Neolithic observatory.

The rocks of Lewis are the oldest in Britain: three billion years old, they are two-thirds the age of the earth. The Callanish Stones are of Lewisian gneiss, a crystalline,

The Stones in silhouette.

granite-like metamorphic rock with distinctive black and white striping and occasional patches of orange. Several stones have small black patches of the mineral hornblend. Some of the natural markings on gneiss can form simulacra – shapes that resemble faces or figures. One of the Callanish Stones has been dubbed 'the Shaman' because of its resemblance to figures seen in Palaeolithic cave paintings.

Callanish's stone circle was constructed between 2,900 and 2,600 BC; it is not known whether the other stones were erected then, or later. The monument fell into disuse sometime around 1,000 BC and eventually became covered with a layer of peat (decayed vegetable matter). In 1857, when only the tops of the tallest stones were visible, the landowner ordered the peat to be cleared and the Callanish Stones were once more revealed.

The Shaman.

Within a mile or so of the Callanish Stones are several more stone circles, some of which are within sight of each other. Callanish III is a beautiful circle of 13 stones, five of which have fallen. The stones are unusual in shape and colour; one is made largely of quartz crystals. Only a short walk from the road, Callanish III is sited on high ground with spectacular views of Loch Roag and the distant mountains. Just a few hundred metres away is Callanish II, and beyond it the majestic Callanish Stones.

Callanish III.

DECORATED STONES

Many standing stones have been decorated in various ways, usually by 'pecking' with a sharp piece of flint to form recessed patterns in the stone. Known generally as 'rock art', the marks take many different forms – the commonest are cup and ring marks. Found all over the British Isles and Europe, the marks are known to be prehistoric but are extremely difficult to date.

Typically, a circular concave depression (cup mark) only a few centimetres across will be surrounded by one or more concentric circles; sometimes a straight line runs out from the centre of the design. There are stones almost entirely covered with cup marks, whereas others have just two or three. Do the marks have some meaning? They may do, but it could be that the process of making them was a ritual act, and that what mattered was not the end result but the process itself.

Ireland has some of the finest rock art in the world. In the Boyne Valley hundreds of large, decorated boulders, or 'kerbstones', surround the huge circular burial mounds of Newgrange, Knowth and Dowth (see opposite). There are many different motifs: spirals, triangles, concentric rings and wavy lines are common, and one stone seems to resemble a complex sundial.

A megalithic triple spiral on the entrance stone at Newgrange.

WHY ERECT STANDING STONES?

It seems that people have always felt the need to erect standing stones. Why should that be? The simplest reason is for permanently marking where territories begin and end, since once it is erected, a stone cannot easily be moved. Neolithic long barrows, as well as being tombs, are thought to have also served as tribal boundaries; usually conspicuously sited in the landscape, they might be visible from miles away. Some standing stones may have served the same purpose. Not all British standing stones are prehistoric, though – some were erected in recent centuries to mark parish boundaries.

A stone axe.

Single standing stones are often found in open areas of moorland. Some could perhaps be way-markers, to guide travellers across the moor. Trade routes were established thousands of years ago in Britain, and stone axes, for instance, were traded widely and transported hundreds of miles. It is quite possible that some standing stones were erected to mark the way for traders.

There may be religious reasons for erecting standing stones. Many traditional cultures share a belief in animism, the oldest of religions. This is the idea that rocks, trees, streams and other features of the landscape possess a spirit, or soul. Before monument building began, earlier prehistoric people very likely venerated certain

Temple Wood Kilmartin.

'special' rocks in their natural state. In one version of animism, human souls reside in inanimate objects after death. Standing stones often resemble human figures, so maybe erecting a stone upright in the ground was a way of acknowledging the human soul within it?

The Easter Island heads are thought to represent the faces of deified ancestors. On excavation their bodies, hidden underground, were found to be decorated with markings.

Stones have always been used to help us, and future generations, to remember significant events or people. There are several accounts in the Bible of standing stones being erected in remembrance. Moses, for instance, after receiving the Ten Commandments, 'builded an altar under the hill, and twelve pillars'.

The permanence of stone makes it particularly suitable for memorials – reminders that should last forever. Today, we place monuments of dressed and polished stone in cemeteries, in remembrance of those who have died: war memorials are actually inscribed with the words: 'lest we forget'. In Madagascar, and other parts of the world, ancient traditions continue as they always have and natural, unworked stones are still erected in memory of the dead. And many look exactly like Britain's prehistoric standing stones.

A British graveyard of stones acting as individual memorials.

HOW WAS IT DONE?

Prehistoric people were capable of incredible feats of engineering. In Brittany, France, the Grand Menhir Brisé was erected in about 4,700 BC. Twenty metres (68 feet) high, it weighed an unbelievable 330 tonnes, yet was somehow transported several miles from where it was quarried and then raised vertically. To move such an enormous piece of stone without breaking it would be barely possible using modern machinery. While this is an extreme example, many stones weighing over 40 tonnes were moved around, erected, and balanced on top of other stones in Neolithic Britain. How did they do it?

The builders probably needed little more than a good supply of timber, rope and ingenuity; their most powerful tool was probably the lever. To quote Archimedes, the great Greek mathematician and engineer: 'Give me a lever long enough and a fulcrum on which to place it, and I will move the earth.'

It is often thought that the stones were dragged along on wooden rollers, but this is impractical for many reasons. Who would attempt to stop a 40-tonne stone from sliding out of control down a hill? A safer way to move very large stones quickly and easily is with levers. The stone is placed on thick, rough timber runners, with more timbers on either side as fulcrums. People are arranged on either side of the stone with their levers positioned under it, synchronising their movements in a rowing motion to lift the stone, move it forward a foot or so, then lower it again onto the runners. The runners and fulcrum timbers are moved forward as the stone progresses. This technique works well on slopes or flat ground.

On the island of Nias, off the western coast of Sumatra, Indonesia, large stones were used to commemorate important deceased people. This photograph captures a stone being hauled upwards – apparently it took 525 people three days to erect it.

Prehistoric people probably used levers to erect stones.

A hole is prepared at the erection site to receive the base of the stone. Stone sockets are dug with a sloping ramp on one side, reinforced with timber 'anti-friction stakes', to guide the stone into its hole. The stone is then raised to vertical by using levers, and ropes suspended from a timber A-frame. The stone is then secured by ramming packing material around its base, and back-filling it to the ground surface.

Capstones and lintels may have been raised into place by dragging them up an earth ramp. However, it is far easier and quicker to use levers to raise the horizontal stone a little at a time, insert supporting timbers, and then raise it more. This process is repeated until the stone reaches the height of its vertical supporting stones, where it is levered into its final position.

FEELING THE VIBES

Since the New Age movement began in the 1960s, standing stones and megalithic monuments have become increasingly associated with strange experiences; a surprising number of people report that they feel some kind of 'energy' from megaliths. Touching standing stones, for some, produces a 'tingling' sensation; a 'swirling' effect is sometimes felt, particularly when moving between a pair of stones. These effects are attributed to mysterious lines of energy that flow through the earth and interact with standing stones.

The Rollright Stones, a stone circle in Oxfordshire, is one of many popular destinations for people who use dowsing rods to detect the 'earth energies' said to flow through prehistoric monuments. Exploring megalithic sites with dowsing rods can be extremely interesting and most people are able to dowse to some degree. There are professional dowsers in Britain who are paid for

Celtic druids bathe in the sunrays shining through the standing stones at Stonehenge.

Druids at Stonehenge.

The Rollright Stones.

their ability to accurately locate water beneath the ground, even specifying the depth. It has been claimed that all megalithic sites are located over underground water, so is that perhaps what is being dowsed? Could this account for the odd effects that people report, or are they caused by some form of electricity?

Many standing stones contain quartz, a common mineral that can form beautiful transparent crystals. Prehistoric builders often favoured stones with prominent areas of quartz, particularly for stone circles. Quartz has unusual electrical properties. When quartz crystals are squeezed, bent or struck they produce a voltage; the piezo-electrical effect has many commercial uses, from electronic clocks to barbecue lighters. Prehistoric people were probably aware that quartz can also produce light. Rub two quartz pebbles firmly against each other in the dark, and the quartz may be seen to glow a dull yellow.

Electrical currents flow through the surface of the earth. When Victorian inventors experimented with earth batteries, they found that inserting two probes of different metals into the ground would produce about one volt of electricity. However, when the probes were arranged north–south, a higher voltage resulted. This phenomenon is now attributed to Telluric Currents – a natural flow of electricity produced by the earth's magnetic field; the strongest currents flow in lines from south to north. If standing stones rich in quartz are inserted into ground where these currents flow, could this maybe account for the 'tingles' and other strange effects that so many people feel when near megaliths?

A stone made of quartz at Boscawen-un.

PLACES TO VISIT

Arbor Low Stone Circle and Gib Hill Barrow
Monyash, Derbyshire, England, DE45 1JS
www.english-heritage.org.uk/visit/places/arbor-low-
stone-circle-and-gib-hill-barrow/

**Avebury (stone circle and avenue; Silbury Hill;
West Kennet long barrow)**
Marlborough, Wiltshire, England, SN8 1RF
www.english-heritage.org.uk/visit/places/avebury/

**Barclodiad y Gawres Burial Chamber
(with decorated stones)**
Ty Croes, Anglesey, North Wales, LL63 5TE
http://cadw.gov.wales/daysout/barclodiad-burial-
chamber/

Boscawen-un (stone circle)
Near St Buryan, Cornwall, England

**Brú na Bóinne (the chambered tombs of
Newgrange, Knowth and Dowth)**
The Boyne Valley, Co. Meath, Ireland
www.worldheritageireland.ie/bru-na-boinne/

Bryn Celli Ddu Burial Chamber (with rock art)
Anglesey, North Wales, LL61 6EQ
http://cadw.gov.wales/daysout/bryn-celli-ddu-burial-
chamber/

Castlerigg Stone Circle
Castle Lane, Underskiddaw, Keswick, Cumbria, England,
CA12 4RN
www.english-heritage.org.uk/visit/places/castlerigg-
stone-circle/

Clava Cairns (stone monuments with rock art)
Inverness, Scotland, IV2 5EU
www.visitscotland.com/info/see-do/clava-cairns

Drombeg Stone Circle
Glandore, West Cork, Co. Cork, Ireland
www.discoverireland.ie/Arts-Culture-Heritage/drombeg-
stone-circle/

Grange Stone Circle
Lough Gur, Co. Limerick, Ireland

Hurlers Stone Circles
Minions, Liskeard, Cornwall, England, PL14 5LE
www.english-heritage.org.uk/visit/places/hurlers-stone-
circles/

Kilmartin Glen (megalithic monuments)
Kilmartin, Lochgilphead, Argyll, Scotland, PA31 8RQ
www.kilmartin.org/

Legananny Dolmen
Dolmen Road, Castlewellan, Banbridge, Co. Down,
Northern Ireland, BT31 9TG

Loughcrew Cairns (with rock art)
Oldcastle, Co. Meath, Ireland

**Ness of Brodgar (Maeshowe chambered tomb;
Neolithic buildings)**
Stenness, Orkney, Scotland
www.visitscotland.com/info/see-do/ness-of-brodgar

Nine Ladies Stone Circle
Stanton Lees, Derbyshire, England
www.english-heritage.org.uk/visit/places/nine-ladies-stone
circle/

The Oxenham Arms Hotel & Restaurant
South Zeal, Dartmoor National Park, nr Okehampton,
Devon, EX20 2JT
www.theoxenhamarms.com

Pentre Ifan Burial Chamber
Nevern, Pembrokeshire, Wales, SA41 3TZ
http://cadw.gov.wales/daysout/pentreifanburialchamber/

Rollright Stones
Stone Ct, Great Rollright, Chipping Norton, England, OX
5QB
www.english-heritage.org.uk/visit/places/rollright-stones/

Standing Stones of Callanish (or Calanais)
Isle of Lewis, Scotland, HS2 9DY
www.callanishvisitorcentre.co.uk/

Stanton Drew Circles and Cove
Stanton Drew, Somerset, England, BS39 4EW
www.english-heritage.org.uk/visit/places/stanton-drew-
circles-and-cove/

Stonehenge
Near Amesbury, Wiltshire, England, SP4 7DE
www.english-heritage.org.uk/visit/places/stonehenge/